Write about your earliest memory.

....

....

....

....

....

....

....

....

Draw what you looked like as a baby.

Draw a picture of your house in the spring.

642 THINGS ABOUT ME

YOUNG WRITER'S & ARTIST'S EDITION

chronicle books · san francisco

ISBN 978-1-4521-5539-5

Manufactured in China.

Design by Eloise Leigh.

10 9 8 7 6 5 4 3 2 1

Chronicle Books LLC
680 Second Street
San Francisco, California 94107

Chronicle Books—we see things differently.
Become part of our community at www.chroniclekids.com.

Chronicle books and gifts are available at special quantity discounts to
corporations, professional associations, literacy programs, and other
organizations. For details and discount information, please contact our
premiums department at corporatesales@chroniclebooks.com or at
1-800-759-0190.

Write about your favorite
rainy-day activity.

....

....

....

....

....

....

....

....

....

....

....

....

....

....

....

....

Draw the different plants
that grow in your neighborhood.

Write a menu for your favorite dinner.

....

....

....

....

....

Write a menu for your least favorite dinner.

....

....

....

....

....

Draw the inside of your refrigerator.

Draw a newspaper with a front-page headline about something that happened to you today.

Draw your front door.

Draw your back door.

Draw the keys to your house.

Where would you hide a secret key?

....

....

....

....

....

....

....

....

Describe your perfect Friday night.

....

....

....

....

....

....

....

....

Draw your pajamas.

Draw your hair when it's messy.

Draw your hair when it's neat.

Draw your most prized possession.

How did you get it?

··

··

··

··

··

··

What do you do with it?

··

··

··

··

··

··

Draw a picture of your bedroom.

Write about all the secret hiding places in your room.

....

....

....

....

....

....

....

....

Draw a picture of your dream bedroom.

Write about a club you
would like to start.

Who would be members?

Draw a logo for your club.

List possible locations for a clubhouse.

....

....

....

....

....

Describe a secret handshake for the club.

....

....

....

....

....

....

Draw the items you pack for a sleepover.

What do you like to do when friends sleep over at your house?

....

....

....

....

....

....

Write about the first time you spent the night away from home.

....

....

....

....

....

....

Write about the latest you ever stayed up.

Write about a time when you were incredibly lucky.

Draw your good luck charm.

Draw a fortune cookie with a fortune you'd like.

Draw the inside of your closet.

Draw what you imagine a friendly monster looks like.

What makes you scared?

....

....

....

....

....

....

How do you overcome a fear?

....

....

....

....

....

....

How do you get to school?

Draw the things you see
on your way to school.

....

....

....

....

....

....

....

....

....

....

....

....

....

....

....

....

What's the first thing you do when you get home from school?

....

....

....

....

....

....

....

....

Draw your favorite after-school snack.

Draw a map of your neighborhood.

Describe your nicest neighbors.

....

....

....

....

....

....

....

....

....

....

....

....

....

....

....

....

....

....

Describe your most mysterious neighbors.

....

....

....

....

....

....

....

....

....

....

....

....

....

....

....

....

....

....

Write about how you get ready for bed.

....

....

....

....

....

....

What do you think about when you're falling asleep?

....

....

....

....

....

Draw what your ceiling looks like when you lie in bed.

Describe a wonderful dream you had.

What games do you play on a long bus or car ride?

....

....

....

....

....

....

....

....

Draw the view out of the window.

Draw all the vehicles your family uses to get around.

Write your name in your fanciest cursive.

....

....

....

....

....

....

....

....

How did your parents choose your name?

....

....

....

....

....

....

....

....

What name would you choose for yourself?

....

....

....

....

....

....

....

What's a nickname you have or a nickname you want?

....

....

....

....

....

....

....

Describe how you lost your first tooth.

....

....

....

....

....

....

....

....

Draw your smile before you
lost your tooth.

Draw your smile after you
lost your tooth.

Draw the view from your bedroom window.

Draw the sky outside of your house during the day.

Draw the sky outside of your house at night.

List all the things that bug you.

List the things YOU do that might bug other people.

....

....

....

....

....

....

....

....

....

....

....

....

....

....

....

....

....

....

What is your favorite subject in school? Why?

....

....

....

....

....

....

....

....

....

....

....

....

....

....

....

....

....

What is your least favorite subject? Why?

....

....

....

....

....

....

....

....

....

....

....

....

....

....

....

....

....

What do you like to do at recess?

....

....

....

....

....

....

Explain the rules of your favorite recess game.

....

....

....

....

....

....

Draw the classmates you'd pick to be on a team with you.

Draw all the pets you know.

Write about an animal you think would make a terrific pet.

Draw the friends you sit with at lunch.

Draw a gigantic sandwich filled with everything you like to eat.

Describe what lunch is like at your school.

....

....

....

....

....

....

Draw a portrait of your parents.

Describe the most embarrassing things they do.

....

....

....

....

....

....

....

....

....

....

....

....

....

....

....

....

....

....

What are you allergic to?

....

....

....

....

....

....

....

....

....

....

....

....

....

....

....

....

Draw yourself sneezing.

Describe how it feels to be sick.

....

....

....

....

....

....

What do you do when you stay home sick?

....

....

....

....

....

....

Draw a magic medicine that makes you feel better.

How would you describe your best friend?

....

....

....

....

....

....

List the ways you are similar.

....

....

....

....

....

List the ways you are different.

....

....

....

....

....

Write about the first time you two met.

....

....

....

....

....

....

....

....

Draw you and your best friend on an adventure.

What do you think is the best part of being an adult?

....

....

....

....

....

....

....

....

What's the worst part?

....

....

....

....

....

....

....

....

Draw a picture of you as an adult.

Describe what you'd like to do when you grow up.

....

....

....

....

....

....

....

....

Write a letter to your future self.

....

....

....

....

....

....

....

....

....

....

....

....

....

....

....

....

....

....

Draw the spot where you do your homework.

Draw the inside of your backpack.

Draw yourself smiling . . .

frowning . . .

laughing . . .

yawning.

Describe a game you and your family play together.

....

....

....

....

....

....

....

....

....

....

....

....

....

....

....

....

....

....

Draw yourself doing your victory dance when you win.

Write about a trip you went on.

....

....

....

....

....

....

Describe the best thing you saw on your trip.

....

....

....

....

....

Describe the strangest thing you saw on your trip.

....

....

....

....

....

Draw a postcard from the place you traveled to.

Draw a postcard from somewhere else you want to visit.

Write about your favorite book.

Draw your favorite place to read.

···

···

···

···

···

···

···

···

···

···

···

···

···

···

···

···

···

Describe how music makes you feel.

....

....

....

....

....

....

Write the chorus to your favorite song.

....

....

....

....

....

Draw a poster of your favorite singer or band.

Write a recipe for something you like to cook.

Draw an invitation to a dinner hosted by you.

Write a guest list for your dinner.

....

....

....

....

....

....

....

....

Draw a clock at the time you wake up.

How do you get ready for school?

....

....

....

....

....

....

....

....

Draw what you love to
eat for breakfast.

Invent a new kind of cereal and
draw the box it would come in.

Write instructions for tying your shoelaces.

....

....

....

....

....

....

....

....

Draw your favorite pair of shoes.

Write a hilarious joke.

....

....

....

....

....

....

....

....

Draw your friends laughing.

Using your right hand, draw your left hand.

Using your left hand, draw your right hand.

Describe your favorite color
and how it makes you feel.

Draw three things in your room
that are your favorite color.

....

....

....

....

....

....

....

....

....

....

....

....

....

....

....

....

....

Draw your grandparents' houses.

How do their houses smell?

··

··

··

··

··

··

Write about your favorite things to do with your grandparents.

··

··

··

··

··

What would you tell a tourist about your hometown?

Describe your favorite thing to do in your town.

....

....

....

....

....

....

....

....

....

Draw what your town looks like from an airplane.

Draw your state flag.

Draw your state bird.

Draw your state flower.

Draw the place where you
keep your money.

Describe how you got your
first dollar bill.

....

....

....

....

....

....

....

....

....

....

....

....

....

....

....

....

....

....

Draw a timeline of a normal day at school.

Draw your favorite animal.

Where does your favorite animal live?

....

....

....

....

....

....

....

....

What does your favorite animal like to eat?

....

....

....

....

....

....

....

....

Draw where your favorite animal sleeps.

Describe a superpower you wish you had.

....

....

....

....

....

....

....

....

Write how your superpower could help others.

....

....

....

....

....

....

....

....

Draw yourself using your superpower.

Write about the first time you went swimming.

....

....

....

....

....

....

....

....

....

....

....

....

....

....

....

....

....

....

Draw your most impressive dive.

What's your favorite swimming stroke? Why is it your favorite?

....

....

....

....

....

How would you teach someone else to swim?

....

....

....

....

....

Draw your nose.

Draw your foot.

Draw your thumbprint.

Draw your shadow.

Write about the family member you have the most fun with.

....

....

....

....

....

....

....

....

Draw an adventure you've had with that person.

Draw the uniform of your favorite sports team.

Write about your favorite sport.

....

....

....

....

....

....

Draw you standing next to your favorite athlete.

Invent a new sport and describe how to play it.

....

....

....

....

....

....

....

....

....

....

....

....

....

....

....

....

....

....

What gives you goosebumps?

....

....

....

....

....

....

....

....

What makes you laugh out loud?

....

....

....

....

....

....

....

....

What makes you nervous?

....

....

....

....

....

....

....

....

What makes you frustrated?

....

....

....

....

....

....

....

....

Write about a time you were in a play or performance.

....

....

....

....

....

....

....

....

....

....

....

....

....

....

....

....

....

....

Write a one-minute play starring you.

Draw the costumes for your play.

What things gross you out?

....

....

....

....

....

....

....

What's the grossest thing you've ever touched?

....

....

....

....

....

....

....

....

What languages do you want to learn to speak?

....

....

....

....

....

....

....

....

Write *hello* in as many languages as you can.

....

....

....

....

....

....

....

....

What would a secret language you made up be called?

....

....

....

....

....

....

....

....

How would you say *hello* and *good-bye* in your language?

....

....

....

....

....

....

....

....

Draw all the kids you sit next to in class.

Draw the view from your desk.

What's your favorite thing to pretend?

....

....

....

....

....

....

Draw what you imagine bears think about.

Draw what you imagine makes trees laugh.

How do you feed your imagination?

....

....

....

....

....

....

....

....

....

....

....

....

....

....

....

....

....

Draw some food your imagination
would eat.

How fast can you run? Draw yourself winning a race.

How slow can you walk? Draw yourself losing a race to a snail.

How high can you jump? Draw yourself jumping over a skyscraper.

How far can you jump? Draw yourself jumping across the Grand Canyon.

What's your favorite time of day?

....

....

....

....

....

....

....

....

When does it feel like time speeds up?

....

....

....

....

....

....

....

....

When does it feel like time slows down?

....

....

....

....

....

....

....

....

What would you do if you could stop time?

....

....

....

....

....

....

....

....

Draw what the world would look like if time stopped.

Draw your favorite fruit.

Draw your favorite vegetable.

Draw yourself dressed as your favorite fruit or vegetable.

Draw a seed growing in the soil. What kind of plant will it become?

Describe how to grow a plant.

....

....

....

....

....

....

Where does the food in your grocery store come from?

....

....

....

....

....

Draw a picture of your house in the summer.

Write about your favorite
summertime activities.

....

....

....

....

....

....

....

....

....

....

....

....

....

....

....

....

....

Draw yourself running
through a sprinkler.

Draw a portrait of your favorite teacher.

List all the amazing things found in your classroom.

....

....

....

....

....

....

....

....

Draw who in your class is
most likely to succeed.

Draw who's the class clown.

Draw who's the nicest.

Draw who's the strongest.

Describe a time when someone lied to you.

....

....

....

....

....

Describe a time YOU lied to someone else.

....

....

....

....

....

Do you think it's ever okay to lie?

....

....

....

....

....

Write a tall tale about why you didn't do your homework.

Draw all of the inventions you think will be in the future.

What do you think the city of the future will look like?

....

....

....

....

....

....

....

....

How do you think we'll get from one place to another?

....

....

....

....

....

....

....

....

Describe your last birthday party.

....

....

....

....

....

....

Draw the best gift you received.

Draw a cake you'd like for your next birthday.

Describe a rule you think is unfair.

....

....

....

....

....

....

....

....

....

....

....

....

....

....

....

....

Write about a time when you got in trouble.

....

....

....

....

....

....

....

....

....

....

....

....

....

....

....

....

Write a review of your favorite restaurant.

....

....

....

....

....

....

....

....

Draw the most delicious dish they serve.

What's something you've been dared to do?

....

....

....

....

....

What's something you've dared a friend to do?

....

....

....

....

....

Draw a triple-dog dare.

Draw a mountain of your favorite candy.

List all of the candy you've tried.

....

....

....

....

....

....

....

....

....

....

....

....

....

....

....

....

....

What's a science project you've made?
How did you come up with the idea?

....

....

....

....

....

....

....

....

Draw a model volcano erupting.

Draw a magnetic field.

List some ideas for a scientific
experiment.

....

....

....

....

....

....

....

....

Draw an invention you'd like to make.

What would you call it?

....

....

....

....

....

....

....

....

....

What would it do?

....

....

....

....

....

....

....

....

What would you need to make it?

....

....

....

....

....

....

....

....

When was the first time you saw the ocean?

....

....

....

....

....

....

....

....

Draw a treasure chest at the bottom of the ocean.

Describe a perfect day at the beach.

....

....

....

....

....

....

....

....

....

....

....

....

....

....

....

....

....

....

Draw the biggest building in your town.

Describe what you think happens inside it.

....

....

....

....

....

....

....

....

....

Draw the view from the top.

Write about a time you went camping.

....

....

....

....

....

....

Describe the sounds you heard at night.

....

....

....

....

....

Draw the wild animals you saw.

What makes you bored?

Draw what you think about
when you're bored.

··

··

··

··

··

··

··

··

··

··

··

··

··

··

··

··

··

Describe a business you want to start. What would you call your business?

....

....

....

....

....

....

....

....

What would your office look like?

....

....

....

....

....

....

....

....

Design your business card.

Draw a happy customer.

When was a time you were surprised?

....

....

....

....

....

....

....

....

....

....

....

....

....

....

....

....

....

What are the steps to planning
a great surprise party?

···

···

···

···

···

···

···

···

···

···

···

···

···

···

···

···

···

Draw someone jumping
out of a cake.

Draw a person you miss.

Write about how you met them.

....
....
....
....
....
....
....
....

What would you say to them right now?

....
....
....
....
....
....
....
....

Write about a time when you got something you wished for.

···

···

···

···

···

···

···

···

···

···

···

···

···

···

···

···

How do you stop hiccups?

....
....
....
....
....
....
....
....

A bloody nose?

....
....
....
....
....
....
....
....

Uncontrollable giggles?

....
....
....
....
....
....
....
....

Draw all the places you're ticklish.

What's something you would change about yourself?

....

....

....

....

....

....

....

....

Why do you think you need to change?

....

....

....

....

....

....

....

....

What's something that you collect?

....

....

....

....

....

....

Draw the prize specimen of your collection.

Draw a museum to hold your collection.

Describe a sporting event you've been to.

....

....

....

....

....

....

Draw what you ate.

Write a cheer you could chant.

....

....

....

....

....

....

Write about a time you got lost.

How did you find your way back?

....

....

....

....

....

....

....

....

Draw a compass for finding your way home.

Draw a friend who looks
different than you do.

Write about all the things
you two have in common.

....

....

....

....

....

....

....

....

....

....

....

....

....

....

....

....

....

What's the best compliment
you ever received?

Draw how it made you feel.

···

···

···

···

···

···

···

···

What's the worst put-down
anyone ever said to you?

Draw how it made you feel.

···

···

···

···

···

···

···

···

Write about a time you went to a carnival or fair.

....

....

....

....

....

....

Draw the things you ate.

What carnival games do you like to play?

....

....

....

....

....

....

Draw your favorite carnival or amusement park ride.

Draw a portrait of the president.

What advice would you give the president?

....

....

....

....

....

....

....

....

Write a speech you'd give if you were president.

....

....

....

....

....

....

....

....

....

....

....

....

....

....

....

....

....

List all of the ways you use water.

List the rivers and lakes
near your home.

....

....

....

....

....

....

....

....

....

....

....

....

....

....

....

....

Draw the animals and plants
you might find in them.

How good are you at keeping your promises?

....

....

....

....

....

....

Describe a promise you made to someone.

....

....

....

....

....

....

Draw what a broken promise would look like.

Draw a map of your favorite park.

Describe how grass smells.

....

....

....

....

....

....

....

....

....

Describe how to make
your favorite dessert.

Draw all the ingredients
that go into it.

....

....

....

....

....

....

....

....

....

....

....

....

....

....

....

....

Describe your favorite movie.

....

....

....

....

....

....

Write the best line in the movie.

....

....

....

....

....

....

Draw your favorite movie snacks.

Who do you like to talk to on the phone?

....

....

....

....

....

....

....

....

What's your favorite app?

....

....

....

....

....

....

....

....

Write a text message to a friend who lives far away.

....

....

....

....

....

....

....

....

Draw your favorite emojis.

What do you think makes a good friend?

....

....

....

....

....

....

....

....

Draw a friendship bracelet.

What was a time when you were REALLY embarrassed?

Draw yourself hiding under your covers.

What's something you like to share?

....

....

....

....

....

....

....

....

What's something you don't like to share?

....

....

....

....

....

....

....

....

Write about a special skill you have.

....

....

....

....

....

....

Explain how you learned your skill.

....

....

....

....

....

Draw yourself on stage performing your skill.

Draw the swimming pool you swim in the most.

Draw what you wear in the pool.

Draw what your feet look like underwater.

What is your favorite smell?

....

....

....

....

....

....

What is your least favorite smell?

....

....

....

....

....

Draw what you think those smells might look like.

Describe what it feels like to dance.

....

....

....

....

....

....

....

....

....

....

....

....

....

....

....

....

....

Draw the steps to a dance
that you invent.

What musical instruments
would you like to play?

....

....

....

....

....

....

....

....

List names for a band you could start.

....

....

....

....

....

....

....

....

Draw your band's first album cover.

Draw your band's tour bus.

Draw your brain and write all the thoughts that are inside it.

What's your favorite dip for french fries?

....

....

....

....

....

....

....

....

What's your favorite pizza topping?

....

....

....

....

....

....

....

....

What's your favorite salad dressing?

....

....

....

....

....

....

....

....

Draw a river of your favorite
thing to drink.

If you won a billion dollars, what would you do?

Draw a piggy bank big enough to hold a billion dollars.

Draw your favorite cartoon character.

Draw yourself as a cartoon character.

Describe what your voice sounds like.

....

....

....

....

....

....

List all the people you can impersonate.

....

....

....

....

....

List all the sound effects you can make with your body.

....

....

....

....

....

Draw something you've been saving up to buy.

How long will it take to save enough money?

....

....

....

....

....

....

What are some ways you could earn more money?

....

....

....

....

....

....

Make a musical playlist
for a friend.

Draw a ticket for a concert
you want to attend.

···

···

···

···

···

···

···

···

···

···

···

···

···

···

···

···

···

What's the best thing about growing up?

....

....

....

....

....

....

....

....

What's the worst thing about growing up?

....

....

....

....

....

....

....

....

What advice would you give someone younger than you?

What's your favorite flavor?

....

....

....

....

....

....

What's a flavor you can't stand?

....

....

....

....

....

Draw three foods with flavors that go really well together.

Describe how to ride a bicycle.

....

....

....

....

....

....

How old were you when you learned to ride a bike? Was it fun? Were you nervous?

....

....

....

....

....

Draw a colossal bike ramp.

What does your name mean? Do you think the meaning of
your name fits you? Why or why not?

....

....

....

....

....

....

....

....

Draw all the hats you own.

Draw yourself wearing
bunny ears.

Draw yourself wearing
a cowboy hat.

Draw yourself wearing a magnificent crown.

Write about a camp you've been to.

....

....

....

....

....

....

....

....

What's your favorite camp activity?

....

....

....

....

....

....

....

....

Draw a campfire.

Draw a gooey s'more.

Write about a time when you broke something valuable.

....

....

....

....

....

....

Write about something you fixed.

....

....

....

....

....

....

Draw all the tools you know how to use.

How do you come up with creative ideas?

....

....

....

....

....

....

....

....

Draw what you imagine an idea looks like.

Draw how you look when
you walk on tiptoe . . .

when you skip . . .

when you stomp your feet . . .

when you moonwalk.

Draw your night-light.

Draw your bedroom with the lights off.

List all the forms of transportation you've ridden on.

Draw yourself riding on a double-decker bus.

Draw yourself flying an airplane.

Draw yourself in the caboose of a train.

How many times can you jump rope?

···

···

···

···

···

···

···

···

···

How many push-ups can you do?

···

···

···

···

···

···

···

···

How many jumping jacks?

···

···

···

···

···

···

···

···

Draw yourself jumping double Dutch
with two friends.

How often do you write in your diary?

....

....

....

....

....

....

Where do you hide your diary?

....

....

....

....

....

....

Draw a fancy burglar alarm for your diary.

Describe your favorite myth or legend.

....

....

....

....

....

....

....

....

....

....

....

....

....

....

....

....

....

Draw your favorite mythical creature.

What's a world record you want to break?

....

....

....

....

....

....

....

....

....

Draw yourself as the yo-yo champion of the world.

What does a healthy planet mean to you?

....

....

....

....

....

....

What can you do to help clean up the Earth?

....

....

....

....

....

Draw the world's biggest mop giving the planet a good scrub.

What's the goal of your favorite video game?

....

....

....

....

....

....

Draw the main character.

Draw what you would look like as a video game character.

If you could live in the world of any book, movie, TV show, or video game, where would you live? Why?

Draw a picture of your house in autumn.

Describe how autumn smells.

Draw an idea for your next
Halloween costume.

···

···

···

···

···

···

···

···

···

···

···

···

···

···

···

···

···

···

Draw yourself on the first day of school.

How does meeting new people feel?

....

....

....

....

....

....

List all the questions you could ask a new friend.

....

....

....

....

....

....

Draw an outfit you love to wear.

How do you feel when
you wear it?

....

....

....

....

....

....

....

....

....

Draw an outfit you don't
like to wear.

How do you feel when
you wear it?

....

....

....

....

....

....

....

....

....

Describe a book you want to write.

....

....

....

....

....

....

....

....

....

....

....

....

....

....

....

....

....

....

Draw a portrait of the main character in your book.

Write about a time that someone was mean to you.

....

....

....

....

....

....

....

....

Draw yourself giving that person a high five.

Write about a time when you were mean to someone.

....

....

....

....

....

....

....

....

Draw a gift you'd like to give to that person.

What's a new subject you think your school should teach?

....

....

....

....

....

....

List people you could talk to to find out more about it.

....

....

....

....

....

....

Draw the cover of a textbook on the subject.

Describe your favorite thing to do in gym class.

....

....

....

....

....

What other ways do you get exercise?

....

....

....

....

....

Draw yourself stretching like rubber.

Write the spookiest story you've heard.

....

....

....

....

....

....

....

....

....

....

....

....

....

....

....

....

....

....

Draw a creepy haunted house you could make for your friends.

What's your favorite season of the year?

....

....

....

....

....

....

What's your favorite thing to do in that season?

....

....

....

....

....

....

Draw yourself jumping into a big pile of leaves.

What would you like to write a blog about? What would it be called?

....

....

....

....

....

....

....

....

Write the first post for your blog.

....

....

....

....

....

....

....

....

If you founded a new country,
what would it be called?

....

....

....

....

....

....

....

....

What would be your country's
national pastime?

....

....

....

....

....

....

....

....

Draw a flag for your country.

Draw a signature dish for
your country.

Write your country's national anthem.

....

....

....

....

....

....

....

....

....

....

....

....

....

....

....

....

....

....

What's a problem you would like to solve?

....

....

....

....

....

....

Describe an invention that could solve your problem.

....

....

....

....

....

....

Draw a blueprint for your invention.

How far can you see?

How close up can you see?

....

....

....

....

....

....

....

....

....

....

....

....

....

....

....

....

Draw a telescope that could
help you see the stars.

Draw a pair of cool sunglasses
you could wear.

Write about a time you accidentally hurt yourself.

....

....

....

....

....

....

....

....

....

....

....

....

....

....

....

....

....

Draw how it happened.

What board games do you play?

....

....

....

....

....

....

....

....

Draw a word search for a friend to solve.

Draw a stormy sky.

Describe what thunder sounds like.

....

....

....

....

....

Describe your family's emergency plan.

....

....

....

....

....

What are your tips and tricks
for climbing trees?

Draw your favorite climbing tree.

....

....

....

....

....

....

....

....

....

....

....

....

....

....

....

....

....

Draw your ultimate tree house.

Draw your toothbrush . . .

your toothpaste . . .

your hairbrush . . .

your fingernail clippers.

Draw your school's mascot. If your school doesn't have a mascot, make one up!

Write a song for your school.

....

....

....

....

....

....

....

....

....

What sorts of things would you grade your parents on?

....

....

....

....

....

....

....

....

Draw a report card for your parents.

Draw one of your
baby pictures.

Draw your favorite family
photograph.

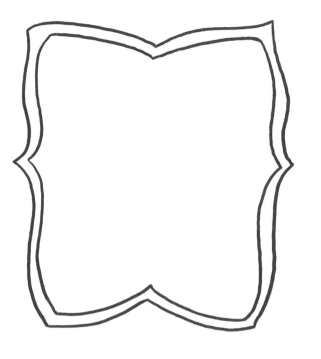

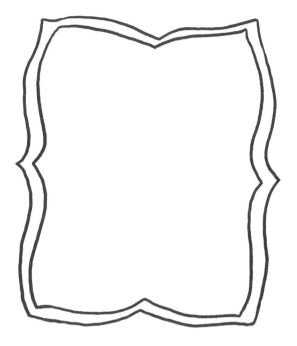

What other words besides "cheese" could you say when getting your picture taken?

....

....

....

....

....

....

....

....

Draw the principal of your school.

What are the rules in your classroom?

....

....

....

....

....

....

How do you feel when you get a good grade?

....

....

....

....

....

....

Draw a campaign poster for yourself running for class president.

Write about how to help your school.

....

....

....

....

....

....

Describe a school holiday you would create.

....

....

....

....

....

....

Describe a mystery you want to solve.

··

··

··

··

··

··

··

··

··

··

··

··

··

··

··

··

··

··

List the main suspects.

....

....

....

....

....

....

Draw one of your fingerprints.

Draw a disguise you could wear while investigating.

Write what you like most about school.

Draw the shortest and tallest
kids in your class.

Draw something that's just
as tall as you.

Draw yourself as tall as a giraffe.

Draw yourself as short as a lemur.

Who's a person you write letters to? Who is someone you'd like to write a letter to?

....

....

....

....

....

Write a short letter to someone in another country.

....

....

....

....

....

Draw a stamp for your letter.

Draw something you've won.

How did you win it?

....

....

....

....

....

....

Draw a trophy you would give yourself.

Draw the toys you played with the most when you were little.

List your favorite books someone read to you when you were little.

Draw everything in your left pocket.

Draw everything in your right pocket.

What's the coolest thing you've ever seen in a museum?

....

....

....

....

....

....

Draw a museum of pancakes.

What other museums do you think there should be?

....

....

....

....

....

....

Draw a valentine for someone you love.

What does loving someone mean?

....

....

....

....

....

....

Describe how love makes you feel.

....

....

....

....

....

....

When was a time that you
were very brave?

....

....

....

....

....

....

....

....

....

....

....

....

....

....

....

....

....

Draw a merit badge for your
act of bravery.

Draw a comic strip about a great day you've had at school.

Describe a trip to your doctor's office.

....

....

....

....

....

....

Draw all the tools your doctor uses.

Draw an x-ray of yourself.

If you could time travel, what time would you travel to?

....

....

....

....

....

....

....

....

Draw the clothes you'd wear to fit in.

Draw what your time machine would look like.

Write about your favorite TV show.

....

....

....

....

....

....

Draw where you sit when you watch TV.

Explain how your family chooses what to watch.

....

....

....

....

....

....

Draw a scene from your favorite TV show.

Draw the biggest animal you've ever seen.

Draw the smallest animal you've ever seen.

Draw the scariest animal you've ever seen.

Draw the furriest animal you've ever seen.

Draw the different rocks you find outside your house.

What does the dirt in your yard smell like?

....

....

....

....

....

....

Draw what you think it looks like a mile underground.

Draw the oldest person in your family.

Write an interesting story that person has told you.

....

....

....

....

....

....

....

....

When was a time you cried?

....

....

....

....

....

....

....

....

....

....

....

....

....

....

....

....

....

Why do you think some people are embarrassed to cry?

....

....

....

....

....

....

....

....

....

....

....

....

....

....

....

....

Draw a teardrop.

What songs do your parents sing?

....

....

....

....

....

....

What songs do you like to sing?

....

....

....

....

....

Draw yourself singing in a band.

Draw all the places you can't reach in your house.

Draw the birds you see in your neighborhood.

Where would you fly if you had wings?

....

....

....

....

....

....

....

....

....

Draw all the places you can crawl under in your house.

What's your proudest moment?

Draw a crowd giving you a standing ovation.

Draw a calendar you could hang in your room.

Write the birthdays of all the people you care about.

....

....

....

....

....

....

....

....

....

....

....

....

....

....

....

....

Describe how you remember important things.

....

....

....

....

....

....

....

....

....

....

....

....

....

....

....

....

Draw the clouds over your house.

Draw the real objects they look like.

Draw a bed made of clouds.

Draw your dentist.

Describe the music that plays in your dentist's office.

....

....

....

....

....

....

....

....

....

What's your favorite place to hang out with friends?

....

....

....

....

....

....

....

....

Why is it such a fun place?

....

....

....

....

....

....

....

....

Draw you and your friends hanging from monkey bars.

Describe what your heartbeat sounds like.

....

....

....

....

....

....

Draw what a thought looks like.

Describe how it feels to take a deep breath.

....

....

....

....

....

....

Draw yourself on the
last day of school.

Draw a last-day bouquet
for your teacher.

How does saying good-bye feel?

....

....

....

....

....

....

....

....

Draw a picture of your house in the winter.

Write about your favorite
winter activities.

....

....

....

....

....

....

....

....

....

....

....

....

....

....

....

....

....

Draw the things you wear
to stay warm.

How do you help out around your house?

....

....

....

....

....

....

Draw your bed when it's messy.

Draw your bed when it's made.

What's the biggest word
you can spell?

....

....

....

....

....

....

....

....

Draw what it means.

What's the biggest number
you can count to?

....

....

....

....

....

....

....

....

Draw what infinity looks like.

Draw what you think the future will look like.

What do you think will be different?

....

....

....

....

....

....

....

....

What do you think will stay the same?

....

....

....

....

....

....

....

....

Draw the funniest person in your family telling a joke.

Draw the smartest person in your family solving a problem.

Draw the nicest person in your family helping you do something.

Draw the bravest person in your family riding a tiger!

What's your theme song?

....

....

....

....

....

What's your catchphrase?

....

....

....

....

....

Draw a piece of clothing that represents your signature style.

Draw the top of your desk.

Draw the underside of your desk.

Draw what the world would look like if you made all the rules.

Draw a historical figure you admire.

Write a famous quote by him or her.

....

....

....

....

....

What question would you like to ask him or her?

....

....

....

....

....

....

Write about an artist who inspires you.

....

....

....

....

....

....

Draw your favorite artwork by that artist.

Describe an art project you would like to do.

....

....

....

....

....

Draw where you go to be alone.

Write about something you've lost.

Draw what it looks like under your bed.

If you built a robot, what would it do?

Draw your robot doing a robot dance.

....

....

....

....

....

....

....

....

....

....

....

....

....

....

....

....

....

....

What do you think is the world's biggest problem?

....

....

....

....

....

....

How would you fix it?

....

....

....

....

....

Draw the tools you would need to fix it.

Draw the top five best presents you've ever received.

If they made a movie about your life, who would play you?

....

....

....

....

....

....

....

....

What about your family members?

....

....

....

....

....

....

....

....

What about your best friend?

....

....

....

....

....

....

....

....

Draw a movie poster for your movie.

Describe what moonlight looks like in your room at night.

....

....

....

....

....

....

Draw the face in the moon.

Draw yourself in an astronaut suit.

Draw all the stars you can see at night.

What do you think aliens from other planets look like?

....

....

....

....

....

....

....

....

What makes you mad?

What makes you sad?

Describe the hottest place you've ever been.

....

....

....

....

....

What did you wear?

....

....

....

....

....

Draw an ice-cold glass of lemonade.

Describe the coldest place you've ever been.

....

....

....

....

....

What did you wear?

....

....

....

....

....

Draw a snowman you'd like to build.

Draw the youngest person in your family.

Write what advice you'd give them as they grow up.

....

....

....

....

....

....

....

....

Draw all the objects you would put inside a time capsule
to represent your life at this moment.

What's your favorite bedtime story?

....

....

....

....

....

....

....

....

Your favorite family story?

....

....

....

....

....

....

....

....

Your favorite story about when you were a baby?

....

....

....

....

....

....

....

....

Draw an illustration for one of your stories.

Write about a time you were bullied.

....

....

....

....

....

Why do you think someone would bully another person?

....

....

....

....

....

How can you stop someone from being bullied?

....

....

....

....

....

Write about how helping
others makes you feel.

Draw someone you
have helped.

....

....

....

....

....

....

....

....

....

....

....

....

....

....

....

....

....

Draw everyone in your family sitting in a humongous tree.

What are your favorite places to shop?

....

....

....

....

....

....

....

....

....

Draw a department-store holiday window display.

What do you think magic looks like?

Describe a spell you think would help others.

....

....

....

....

....

....

Write the magic words you'd say to cast your spell.

....

....

....

....

....

....

What does snow taste like?

....

....

....

....

....

....

....

....

....

What does wind feel like?

....

....

....

....

....

....

....

....

....

What does rain taste like?

....

....

....

....

....

....

....

....

What does sunshine feel like?

....

....

....

....

....

....

....

....

Write about an adventure you'd like to go on.

....

....

....

....

....

....

....

....

Draw what you would need to pack for your adventure.

What does it mean to be healthy?

....

....

....

....

....

....

List things you and your family could do to be healthier.

....

....

....

....

....

....

Draw what you think a germ looks like.

Draw all the gifts you could give your family and friends for their birthdays.

What do you think it
means to be smart?

....

....

....

....

....

....

....

....

....

....

....

....

....

....

....

....

....

Draw the smartest person
you know.

What do you think is the best way to settle an argument?

....

....

....

....

....

....

Write about a time when you were treated unfairly.

....

....

....

....

....

....

Draw rock-paper-scissors.

Draw what you think your great-great-great-great-grandparents looked like.

Write about where your family came from originally.

....

....

....

....

....

....

Draw a family coat of arms.

What was your biggest accomplishment this year?

....

....

....

....

....

....

....

....

....

....

....

....

....

....

....

....

....

Write an hour-by-hour schedule for your perfect day.

Draw the perfect end to your perfect day.

Write about a wedding you've been to.

....

....

....

....

....

....

What would your wedding be like?

....

....

....

....

....

Draw a ten-layer wedding cake.

What are your goals for next year?

....

....

....

....

....

....

....

....

....

....

....

....

....

....

....

....

....

....

What's your favorite holiday?
Why is that holiday important?

....

....

....

....

....

....

....

....

How does your family celebrate?

....

....

....

....

....

....

....

....

Draw a table with all the
holiday foods you eat.

Draw an outfit you wear
on that holiday.

Write a poem about what quiet sounds like.

Draw a comic strip about the funniest thing that's ever happened to you.

What do you think your town looked like a million years ago?

Draw a dinosaur that might have lived in your town.

Draw your library.

Write a story about a magical library book.

List the best things that have happened to you this year.

....

....

....

....

....

....

....

....

....

....

....

....

....

....

....

....

....

Draw your eyes open.

Draw your eyes closed.

Describe what you see when you close your eyes.

....

....

....

....

....

....

Draw the cover of your bestselling autobiography.